BROOKE BESSESEN

look who lives in the desert!

Bouncing and Pouncing, Hiding and Gliding, Sleeping and Creeping

Brooke Bessesen has two equally loved careers.

One entails animals. She spent several years with the Phoenix Zoo medical team as a certified veterinary technician helping treat hundreds of species from anteaters to zebras. Concurrently, she served as the zoo's on-camera naturalist.

Her other career is in television. Brooke created a children's show, **Cool Critters**; wrote wildlife segments for the Emmy-winning series **What's Up**; and produced a top-rated weekly program, **A Brighter Day**.

She currently writes and produces for cable networks, including National Geographic Channel and Discovery.

Look Who Lives in the Desert! is her first book, and she continues to write about the creatures that inspire her. She still participates in Arizona native wildlife rescue efforts as a volunteer.

Brooke lives in Scottsdale, Arizona, with her husband, Kevin, and their dog, Malki.

For my friends who rescue and rehabilitate desert wildlife.
And for my mouse. I love you.

ACKNOWLEDGMENTS
With a happy heart I offer gratitude to all the
wonderful people who helped me bring this book to life:
to those who taught me about animals and fostered
my passion for understanding them;
to my special friends who listened, looked, and encouraged;
to Dad and Dan, for artistic support;
to Grandpa Evans, if you are watching, for teaching me to rhyme;
to Kevin, for sharing the journey and being my partner in creative mischief;
and to everyone at **Arizona Highways** for your enthusiasm and vision.
And my deepest thanks are reserved for Mom, for always being my first-run
editor and for believing since I was 7 that this day would come.

Art Director MARY WINKELMAN VELGOS
Designer AMANDA FARMER
Book Editor BOB ALBANO
Copy Editors EVELYN HOWELL
PK PERKIN MCMAHON
Cover Design MARY WINKELMAN VELGOS
Photography MARTY CORDANO
(EXCEPT PHOTOS OF AUTHOR, KIT FOX, AND GORILLA)

FOR YOUNG IMAGINATIONS and ARIZONA HIGHWAYS are registered trademarks
of the Arizona Department of Transportation, parent of **Arizona Highways**.

Text and Illustrations © 2004 by Brooke Bessesen

Gila monster background on pages 20-21 and cover by Rick Burress

Library of Congress Control Number 2003112982

ISBN-13: 978-1-932082-09-8

ISBN-10: 1-932082-09-3

Published by the Book Division of **Arizona Highways**® magazine,
a monthly publication of the Arizona Department of Transportation,
2039 West Lewis Avenue, Phoenix, Arizona 85009.
Telephone: (602) 712-2200
Web site: www.arizonahighways.com

Publisher WIN HOLDEN
Managing Editor BOB ALBANO
Associate Editor EVELYN HOWELL
Director of Photography PETER ENSENBERGER
Production Director KIM ENSENBERGER
Production Assistant VICKY SNOW

When I began writing **Look Who Lives in the Desert!** I knew I wanted to entertain and educate readers and to share with them my fascination with animals. The desert's wildlife is unique and beautiful, but some species can intimidate people. In an effort to make the desert dwellers less daunting, I opted to create silly characters. After all, it's hard to be afraid of a tarantula when she's wearing a tutu. By viewing a whimsical package along with the facts, young readers may have an easier time relating to the animals and remembering what they've learned.

The writing style is my version of wordplay, which is to say the rhyming is for sheer fun — and to keep readers (and their tongues) alert. My primary concern is sharing information, not necessarily the conventions of poetry.

Characterizing the animals with illustrations was a delightful experience. I used fabrics and real-world textures in my palette and made a point of including little elements for readers of all ages to look for throughout the book.

I chose to add facts about each animal to help explain the rhyming text, keep you (and the animals) safe, and clear up some misconceptions. Plus, I included a few juicy ones not everyone knows (like how vultures stay cool). The facts range from quite simple to a little more complex to offer interesting tidbits for each level of learning. With Marty Cordano's wildlife photographs to complete this scientific facet, you might even use the book to settle a debate or two at the dinner table.

It is my sincere wish that you have a good laugh or at least a chuckle … and that you learn something. Perhaps you will come to love the desert dwellers as much as I do.

— Brooke Bessesen

Some people think

the   is bare,

that nothing would live there,

that no one would dare.

The place would seem

to be barren and bleak,

but if you look closely,

and you sneak a peek,

you'll find many creatures

with features unique.

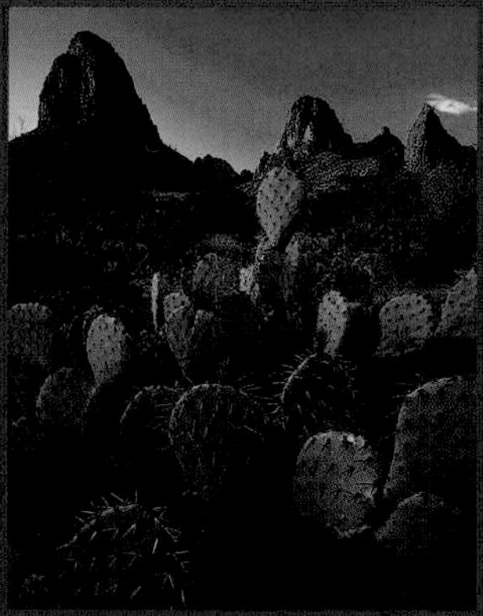

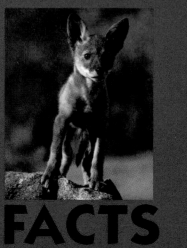
Coyotes are timid,

but they love to sing,

yelping it up in a musical fling.

At dusk, everyone in the choir sits tall,

and the symphony grows

as they each start to call.

It's a wonderful, howling-good concert

for all!

COME SEE THE SHOW...
THE AMAZING GECKO
Tremendous! Stupendous!
De-endous! Re-endous!

ADMISSION
(1) One yummy juicy tasty bug (1)

FASCINATING

FACTS

🦎 Geckos are typically small, nocturnal (active at night) lizards that eat insects. Like snakes, most geckos do not have eyelids, so a clear scale called a spectacle scale protects their eyes.

🦎 Geckos that climb well do so because they have rows of spatula-tipped setae (tiny hairs) that make up large pads on the tips of their toes. These microscopic hairs help them cling to vertical and inverted surfaces.

🦎 Geckos can store fat and water in their tails. When caught by the tail, a gecko can release the tail from its body and run away. A new tail eventually grows back, but sometimes it is

A **gecko** does magic.
He has a great act:
He can lose his long tail,
then make it grow back!

Plus, he has a trick that is
quite hard to beat:
He walks upside down
without suction-cup feet,
just looking for something
that's tasty to eat.

KNOWN WORLDWIDE
for this
DEATH-DEFYING FEAT
with his
INCREDIBLE FEET
...DON'T MISS IT!

shorter than the previous one.

⚹ Most lizards cannot make sounds, but geckos have vocal cords and can produce sharp chirps or squeaks when startled.

⚹ Geckos have soft, colorful, often translucent skin. They use their tongues to keep their eyes clean and moist.

⚹ Although wall-climbing geckos often are seen in desert artwork, the most common gecko in the Southwest is the banded gecko, which has moveable eyelids, no toe pads, and is mainly terrestrial (stays on the ground).

⚹ People often mistake banded geckos for baby Gila monsters.

- A cactus wren builds a football-shaped nest with the entrance on one side near the top. These wrens usually build their nests in cholla cacti or thorny bushes to discourage predators (like snakes) from getting in to eat the eggs or young hatchlings.
- When males and females pair up, the male builds the nest. He also builds at least one other "dummy" nest to confuse would-be predators. Both parents take care of their young.
- Cactus wrens eat a wide variety of foods, including insects, spiders, some lizards, fruits, and seeds. They even turn over rocks and other objects on the ground with their beaks to look for hiding creatures.
- Cactus wrens take dust baths. Every evening they rub on the ground and kick dirt up into their feathers. Then they shake it off, like a wet dog. This helps them stay clean and get rid of parasites.
- The cactus wren is Arizona's state bird.

In cactus that's prickly,
with spines long and dry,
a little wren flutters
so perky and spry.

She has a great nest site,
it's perfect you see,
since guests can't get in
without knowing the key.
No snakes will be stopping
for cookies and tea.

With grocery-bag cheeks

that can carry a bunch,

a **kangaroo rat**

shops for goodies to munch.

He knows how to pick

the best grasses and seeds

from aisles of shrubs

and sharp, thorny weeds.

His underground pantry

holds extras he needs.

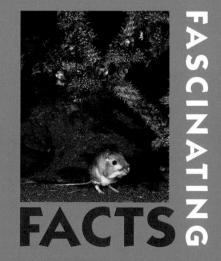

FASCINATING FACTS

FASCINATING FACTS

A *tarantula*
has a soft tiptoeing prance,
like a brown ballerina
in an eight-legged dance.

She lays a silk carpet
on her burrow floor,
so she'll know if a visitor
comes to the door
to join her for dinner —
a feast to be sure!

They are not pigs
even though they are stout,
and each one is blessed
with a rubbery snout.

Sniffing and snorting,
just searching for clues,
to find food and news
Javelina can use,
like desert detectives
with funky hair-dos!

Due to drought, reports indicate that mesquite trees are producing fewer pods. These scrumptious pods, also called mesquite beans, are eaten by so many desert animals that the shortage has browsers worried. Many of this season's pods are already missing, presumably eaten by rodents and birds. Efforts are underway to locate any remaining pods before the

continued on page 6

JAVELINA DAILY

Spring Issue   Volume 23

DBI Attempting to Crack New Case

Local agents from the region's Desert Bureau of Investigation are searching for missing mesquite pods

¤ Javelina are not members of the pig family even though they look similar. They travel in herds of 6 to 30 members. Their coarse, bristly hair helps protect them from the harsh landscape they walk through.

¤ Their true name is collared peccaries (they have namesake "collars" of lighter hair from under their necks to their shoulders), but the common name is javelina because their razor sharp canine teeth resemble an ancient spear-like weapon called a javelin.

¤ Javelina are typically crepuscular (active during dusk and dawn). They are also omnivores

(meat and plant eaters) but they dine mostly on desert vegetation, including mesquite pods and prickly pear cactus.

¤ Each javelina has a scent gland at the top of its rump that secretes an oily, musky substance (very smelly!), which it uses to mark its territory and help keep the herd together.

¤ Javelina have a good sense of smell and can hear fairly well, but they have poor eyesight. Because they cannot see well, they startle easily and may attack in defense. If you see javelina in the wild, move away from them slowly and give them plenty of space.

FASCINATING FACTS

Some of the **bats** that
swoop 'round in the night
fly cactus to cactus
to help keep things right.

Drinking from flowers
that grow up on top,
they sip the sweet nectar
like pop in a shop
and swap precious pollen
wherever they stop.

FASCINATING FACTS

- Most bats eat insects, but a few eat cactus nectar and pollen. Like bees, they are pollinators. This makes them important to the survival of large cacti like the saguaro and certain agave species. When these bats poke their heads into cactus flowers to eat, pollen sticks to the fur on their heads and then rubs off when they go to the next flowers.
- When bats eat cactus fruit, they swallow the seeds, which are later dispersed with their droppings, helping new plants to grow.
- Bats are nocturnal (active at night) and they are the only mammals that actually fly, unlike so-called "flying" squirrels that really just glide.
- Bats are not rodents nor even related to rats. They belong to their own order called Chiroptera, which means "hand-wing."
- Bats are not blind. They have good eyesight, but they mostly use echolocation, like dolphins, a process of sending out sound waves. The sound waves bounce off objects and come back to give them a three-dimensional sense of their surroundings in the dark.

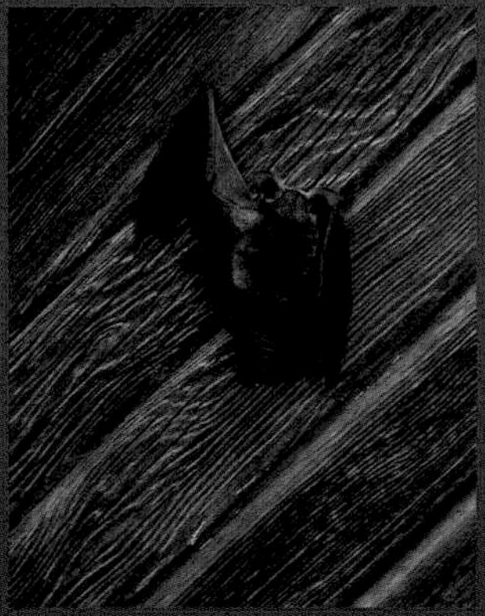

FASCINATING

FACTS

Gila monster

is certainly one to discuss,

she's pretty, but she's also venomous!

You'll know that it's her

by the skin on her back,

with bumps like the beads

on an old woman's sack

in Halloween colors

of bright orange and black.

If you look upward into a blue sky,

you might see a **hawk**

soaring ever so high.

She glides on the breeze

with such ease — like a kite.

What a wonderful vision,

a glorious sight,

to behold this great bird

taking feathers to flight!

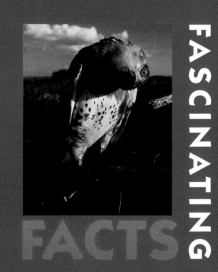

FASCINATING FACTS

He travels as much

as a businessman might

and he's not a bother,

he's very polite.

But little *stink*

beetle is always alone

because when he's scared

he starts squirting cologne!

And the smell

seems to, well . . .

make everyone groan.

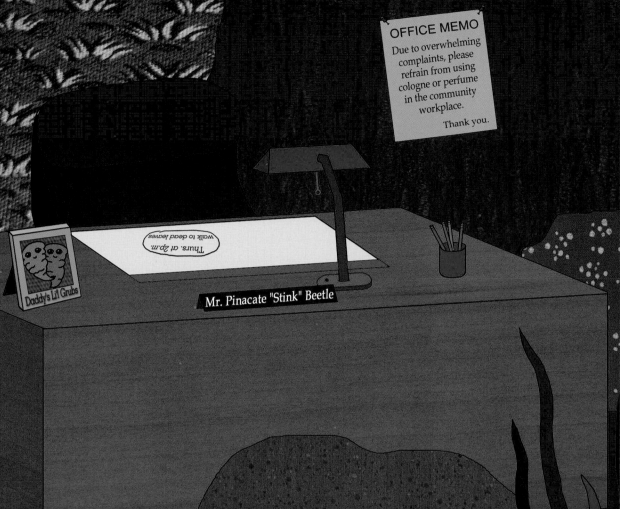

OFFICE MEMO

Due to overwhelming complaints, please refrain from using cologne or perfume in the community workplace.

Thank you.

Thurs. at 2 p.m.
walk to dead leaves.

Daddy's Li'l Grubs

Mr. Pinacate "Stink" Beetle

◎ Beetles are the most populous group of insects on the Earth.
◎ Another name for the stink beetle is pinacate beetle. (Pinacate is derived from the Aztec word **pinacatl** meaning "black beetle.") Sometimes it is also called a clown beetle because of its comical habit of doing a headstand when it senses danger.

◎ Like all insects, the stink beetle has six legs and three body segments: head, thorax, and abdomen. It breathes through tiny openings along its abdomen called spiracles.

JUNE

		1	2	3	4	5	6
7	8	9	10	11	12	13
14	15	16	17	18	19	20
21	22	23	24	25	26	27
28	29	30	Stink travels all month

Nature Happens

The Desert

FREQUENT NON-FLYER

GO BUGGY

P.U. COLOGNE

FASCINATING FACTS

◎ Stink beetles have glands at the end of the abdomen that produce a repulsive-smelling liquid. They can squirt this fluid to discourage predators from disturbing or attacking them. Some larger species can shoot this reddish-black liquid up to 20 inches.

◎ The stink beetle cannot fly — its elytra (wing covers) are fused, and its flying wings are missing. Instead, it runs with its head down and its backside sticking up at about a 45-degree angle.

◎ Finding food by scent, stink beetles primarily eat decaying vegetation and seeds from desert plants.

The number of desert tortoises in the wild has dropped dramatically, and they are a threatened species, so it is very important never to touch or pick up a wild tortoise! Only look.

Tortoises use their shells for protection and can pull their head and legs inside to hide from predators.

Tortoises are herbivores (vegetarians) and eat a wide variety of desert plants, including flowers, grasses, cactus pads, and fruit. They can drink large amounts of water at one time and then go extended periods before drinking again.

To escape the desert's extreme heat and cold, tortoises spend most of their time in underground burrows. Their forelegs, which are flatter than the hind legs and have hard, protective scales and clawed feet, are designed for digging.

Tortoises do not have teeth; rather, their jaws are sharp and serrated to cut through the tough vegetation they eat.

The carapace (top shell) of an adult desert tortoise is 9 to 15 inches long, and the dome is 4 to 6 inches high. The male's plastron (under shell) is concave, while the female's is flat.

Some tortoises live to be 80 years old or older.

FASCINATING

FACTS

She plods along slowly,

her house on her back.

It's not very fancy —

a scaled shell shack.

This good-natured

tortoise   is just on her way.

The desert buffet

offers nothing gourmet

but she loves a nice stroll

on a beautiful day.

The roadrunner darts
with incredible speed.
As he comes from the thicket,
he's out in the lead!

He really can't fly,
but those skinny legs move,
and the shape of his feet
would be hard to improve.
No one outruns him
when he's in the groove!

- A roadrunner's feet are zygodactyl (two toes facing forward and two toes facing back). Their toes form an X for good standing balance.
- Roadrunners can fly, but not very well, so they usually just run on the ground, using their foot-long tail to help them turn and stop quickly, like the rudder and flaps on an airplane. As small as they are, roadrunners can travel at speeds over 15 mph!
- Roadrunners don't eat seeds. They prefer insects, spiders, and small animals like mice and lizards. They kill their prey by stabbing it with their 2-inch beaks. Roadrunners even catch and eat rattlesnakes!
- If a predator gets too close to its nest, the roadrunner performs a convincing "broken leg" act to lure the predator away. Roadrunners pair for life, and both parents care for the young.
- The roadrunner is New Mexico's state bird.

FASCINATING FACTS

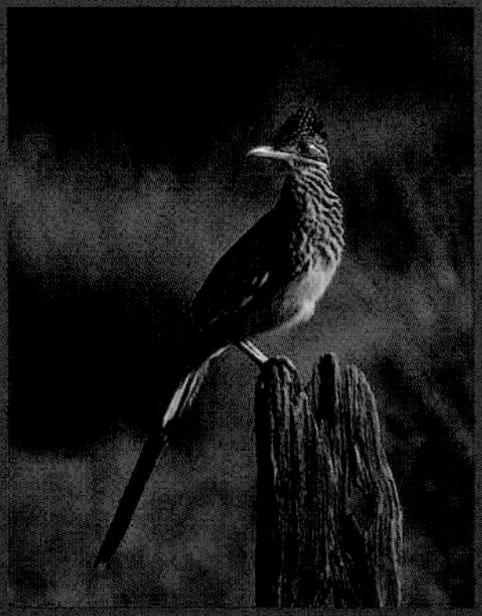

The **Cougar**
is resting like a royal queen.
Her lion eyes gaze.
Her paws are licked clean.

She weighs almost 100
pounds — even more
but unlike the King of old
legends and lore,
she's called a "small" cat
because she can't roar.

Sir Lion of Mountains VII

Desert Dwellers
Claw Care for Dummies (The Royal Family)
The King and I
The Lion Queen
The Purr-fect Girl
Big Book of MEOW-ALONGS
The Deer Hunter
The Carnivore
Prey for the Felines
Cat on a Hot Tin Roof
SCRATCH-N-SNIFF
CATS
Eight Ways to Catch a Mouse
The Puma Princess

The cougar has more than 40 common names, including mountain lion, puma, catamount, painter, and panther.

Cougars are the most widely distributed cat in the Americas. Once, they ranged from coast to coast in North America, but their population has declined, and they now are found in limited areas.

When they are full-size, cougars weigh 80 to 200 pounds. Males are bigger than females. Cougars can live as long as 20 years.

A cougar cannot roar like an African lion because the bones in the cougar's voice box are too small and tightly connected. Instead, it

makes a purring sound. For this reason it is considered a "small cat" despite its large physical size.

❖ Cougars typically live in mountainous or rocky terrain and hunt deer, elk, and small animals. They have retractable claws so they run silently.

❖ They are considered to be nocturnal (active at night), but they might hunt during the day, especially if prey is scarce.

❖ Because their hind legs are longer than their front legs, they are tremendously powerful jumpers. They can leap up to 18 feet from a standstill!

❖ Most cats have eye pupils that retract to a slit, but cougars' pupils stay round.

FASCINATING

SIDE FACTS

Vultures eat carrion (the remains of dead animals). If there were no vultures cleaning up dead things, there could be dangerous levels of bacteria that might make people and other animals very sick.

Vultures have bald heads so they don't get messy feathers when they reach into a carcass to eat. If threatened on the ground, vultures sometime regurgitate (throw up) to drive away the intruder and make themselves lighter for flight.

When vultures soar, they use their excellent eyesight to look for carrion. They also have big nostrils and can smell carrion up to 50 miles away.

Soaring vultures get lift from thermals (invisible updrafts of warm air) and can be recognized by their V-shaped wing position called a dihedral. Vultures can have wingspans of up to 6 feet.

Because they can't sweat, vultures sometimes dribble pee on their legs to help them cool off in hot temperatures. This process has a big name — ureohydrosis.

FASCINATING

FACTS

Vultures are special.
Their job is distinct.
Without their strange cravings,
we might be extinct.

They look from the skies for more
waste to be had.
They eat things so yucky!
They eat things so bad!
You'd think from the stink they'd
gone utterly mad!

A **kit fox** has ears
too big for his size,
but they help him stay cool
when the temperatures rise.

His dark basement bedroom
is easy to keep;
it's in a round burrow
that's slender and deep.
He spends the hot days there
asleep in a heap.

❂ Kit foxes are rarely seen, especially because they are nocturnal (active at night) and sleep during the day.
❂ The kit fox's large ears let off heat to help the fox lower its body temperature. They also give the fox excellent hearing.
❂ Foxes either dig their own burrows or use old ones from other animals. The burrows may measure up to 15 feet long and lie 5 feet below the surface of the ground. Burrows are usually round inside and have multiple entrances.
❂ Kit foxes weigh 3 to 6 pounds, about the size of an average house cat. They have slender legs and a long, bushy tail.
❂ A dog-family member, the kit fox is the second-smallest dog. (The fennec fox in northern Africa is the smallest.)
❂ The kit fox mostly eats rodents; it also feeds on insects, fruits, and grasses.
❂ Non-retractable claws on their four-toed feet give them good traction for running. They also have fur on the bottom of their feet to protect them from the hot desert sand.
❂ Kit foxes prefer to live in open, sandy, level terrain with low desert vegetation, and they mate for life. A mother gives birth between February and May to a litter of three to seven pups, and both parents care for the young.

FASCINATING

FACTS

In a steep canyon,
out on a red butte,
bighorns like a
model in a photo shoot.

With horns that curl back
in a style so slick,
she's regal and lovely;
but she's also quick,
with sheep shoes that
make a sharp clickity-click.

TODAY's
FASHION SHOOT
is for
Butte-E MAGAZINE

Please try not to
startle Miss Bighorn

Bighorn sheep live in family groups on rocky ridges, cliffs, and buttes. Males and females live separately most of the year.

Both males and females have horns, but the males' are much bigger and can even curl all the way around when they get older. Males' horns can weigh up to 30 pounds. A bighorn uses his horns for head-to-head fighting with other males for mating rights.

Bighorns can maneuver amazingly well on narrow cliffs, easily leaping from one little ledge to another, sometimes ones only 2 inches wide. The outer edges of their hooves

are hard, to help them stand on tiny projections of rock; but the soles of their feet are soft, to help them cling to smoother surfaces and to soften the impact when they jump. Bighorns can leap a span of nearly 20 feet!

Bighorn sheep have very acute eyesight. Their good peripheral vision (out to the sides) and depth perception help them move about on mountainsides without falling. Their long-distance sight allows them to see potential predators getting too close.

Bighorns eat desert vegetation and can go extended periods without water. They live an average of 15 to 20 years.

FASCINATING FACTS

The bobcat is also known as the red lynx or the wildcat.

Tufts of hair on the tips of a bobcat's ears may act as antennae to aid in hearing.

A bobcat has a short tail and weighs 20 to 30 pounds.

Bobcats are mainly nocturnal (active at night). They are also carnivores (meat-eaters) and eat small prey including rabbits, rodents, birds, and sometimes deer or sheep.

Their mottled or spotty coloring creates what is called camouflage (looks like its surroundings), making them hard to see. By blending in, they can sneak up on their prey more easily.

Adult bobcats live alone in rocky terrain and areas with dense vegetation. They are excellent tree climbers and swimmers and may travel up to 20 miles a night for hunting.

Like other cats, bobcats can see well at night. A shiny layer of cells behind the retina called the **tapetum lucidum** (Latin for "bright carpet") reflects light back through the retina and improves low-light vision. This is also what makes their eyes shine at night.

FASCINATING FACTS

With blotches that look
like a tan army vest,
a bobcat blends in
to the Desert Southwest.

The noises nearby
can come in LOUD and clear
because he has hair tufts
that grow from each ear
like little antennas
that help him to hear.

One desert babe
has a *rattle* to shake.
She's young for a *snake*,
but make no mistake!

She's quite easygoing,
a lady with grace,
as long as no one tries
to get in her face
as she rests by a rock
in her favorite place.

/\/\/\ Rattlesnakes are very venomous and should never be touched or handled! They are not generally considered aggressive toward people, but can deliver a severe bite if frightened.

/\/\/\ Rattlesnakes shake their tails to express that they feel threatened. They are born with a "button" on the tip of their tails. Each time they shed their skins, they get one more button. The dry, loosely connected buttons make a buzzing sound when rattled.

/\/\/\ Rattlesnakes have a good sense of smell, but they also use their tongues to determine their surroundings. The forked tip picks up particles in the air and then places them into a small sensory organ in the roof of the snake's mouth, called the Jacobson's Organ.

/\/\/\ Rattlesnakes hear and see poorly, but they have two pits between their nostrils and eyes that help them detect temperature changes. They use these receptors to find small animals they eat.

/\/\/\ Rattlesnakes are 'ovoviviparous' (the female holds fertilized eggs inside her while the babies grow). Once the young are fully developed, she deposits them in thin membranes that immediately break, giving the impression of a live birth.

FASCINATING

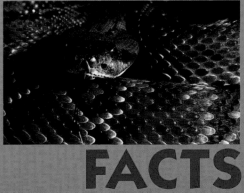

FACTS

FASCINATING FACTS

The desert night watchman

sits perched in a tree

with big, yellow owl eyes

that help him to see.

Turning his head

three-quarters around,

he listens intently

to every new sound,

especially a rustle

from down on the ground.

Under a rock

hiding deep in a crack,

a *scorpion* carries

her young on her back.

Thirty small kiddies

all sitting so sweet:

Each with two pinchers

and eight tiny feet

and a stinging utensil

when it's time to eat.

≷ Scorpions are venomous and should never be touched or handled! They are not considered aggressive, but they may sting in self-defense.

≷ Like spiders, scorpions have 8 legs. They also have 2 pinchers called pedipalps that they use like hands. Even with multiple eyes, scorpions have terrible eyesight. A scorpion uses its stinger to inject venom into its prey: insects, spiders, and even other scorpions.

≷ Scorpions have many babies at a time, 30 on average. The baby scorpions are born live and climb up to ride on their mother's back. They stay on her for 7 to 10 days before they go off on their own.

≷ Scorpions spend the day in dark places — under rocks, etc. — and hunt at night. They remain relatively inactive during winter months when nighttime temperatures drop below 77 degrees Fahrenheit.

≷ A scorpion's exoskeleton (the body's hard, armorlike outer surface) appears to glow green under ultraviolet (black) light.

Jackrabbit's
feet are amazing, it's true.
They're as long as his ears
and they're powerful, too!

He thumps like a drum when
he starts to feel fear.
It's his way to say: Look out!
Danger is near!
Then he springs out of sight
with his rump in high gear!

With especially long earlobes, jackrabbits have excellent hearing. They also move their ears for temperature control: up to cool off, and down at night to retain heat.

Jackrabbits sometimes thump their back feet on the ground to warn others of danger.

When panicked, jackrabbits can hop up to 20 feet in one leap and travel at speeds of 30 to 35 mph in a zigzagging pattern to avoid predators.

Jackrabbits are mainly nocturnal (active at night) and eat desert vegetation including grasses and the leaves of bushes. Sometimes jackrabbits eat their

Rock
-n-
Rabbit

Rock-n-Rabbit's Greatest Hits
with the smash hit single
'Run for Your Life'

CDs
AVAILABLE
HERE

own droppings in order to get all the moisture out of the dry foods they eat.

◎ Despite their name, jackrabbits are actually hares. Unlike rabbits, hares are born covered in fur and with their eyes open.

◎ Jackrabbits rarely dig burrows, and a female has her young above ground in a shallow, often fur-lined, depression. They breed year-round, and have an average of two to four litters each year

with two to five leverets (young hares) in each litter.

◎ Large eyes on the side of its head allow a jackrabbit to see nearly 360 degrees around itself to watch for predators.

FASCINATING FACTS

So you see, the desert
is really not bare,
that animals live there,
yes, so many dare!

It's like a big family
that can't work apart.
Some creatures are athletes
while others are smart,
but each is a work of art
with a *heart!*